Piercing the Heart
POEMS BY
Yunus Emre

TRANSLATED BY
JESSE CROSSEN

Piercing the Heart
Copyright © 2022 by Jesse Crossen
This edition was compiled July 8, 2022

© ⓘ ⓢ

This work is licensed under the Creative Commons
Attribution-ShareAlike 4.0 International License.
To view a copy of this license, visit
http://creativecommons.org/licenses/by-sa/4.0/
or send a letter to
Creative Commons,
PO Box 1866,
Mountain View, CA 94042, USA.

ISBN 979-8-83-566727-7

Design and illustrations by Jesse Crossen

HINTERLANDER
500 Westover Dr #16346
Sanford, NC 27330
https://hinterlander.substack.com

Contents

Notes	4
Invocation	16
One Word	18
Spring	20
It Comes and Goes	23
I Need It Back	24
That Pearl	25
Let Down Thy Veil	26
You're the One for Me	27
Going Home	29
Hey Loverboy	30
Lying Down	32
Crying	33
I Came	34
Poison	36
Let There Be Separation	37
You Can't	38
What's Wrong With Me	39
Come See	40
The Hour of Death	42
If That's the Way	44
Mine	45
Inside of Me	46
Oh Nightingale	48
I Don't Have any Wish to Fly	49
Life Slips Through our Fingers	50
Plundered	52
Thanks	54

About the Poet

Yunus Emre was born in 1238 in Anatolia, a region of what is now Turkey, and died around 1320. He followed a mystical and freethinking branch of Islam called Sufism, but he had little interest in sectarian differences. He was one of the first to compose poetry in the everyday Turkish of his people rather than in Persian or Arabic, and his poems were really folk poetry, in the same sense as folksongs and folktales. Long before they were printed in books, they were passed along by word of mouth, recited at gatherings of religious orders and laypeople and sung as songs and hymns. Over 700 years later, he remains one of the most beloved poets in the Turkish language, seen by many as a folk hero and a saint. Not much is known about the details of his life, but his work reveals a fascinating character: a tortured soul, a biting wit, a self-deprecating humor, a tough love for humanity, an ecstatic love for God, and a deep current of divine inspiration. Just like us, Yunus lived in a time of upheaval and rapid change, and his poems have a vital message, showing us that reaching out for the divine can be both an escape from the world's struggles and an all-consuming struggle of its own. His intense and uncompromising humanism speaks to people in all times, all places, and all walks of life.

Translation Notes

Languages and cultures are profoundly different, and this means there's no such thing as a perfect translation. Instead, a translator has to make sacrifices and set priorities that help decide what to sacrifice. Some people prefer a literal rendering, some like a learned one, some like a beautiful one. My priorities are:

1. Be faithful to the underlying message. This is the essence of what Yunus was trying to get across and the reason he wrote poems at all. If I lose his message or distort it too much, I've failed. Unfortunately I'm limited by my ability to understand, but that's an inescapable part of the human condition.

2. Speak plainly and naturally. This makes the poems accessible to a wider audience, and also makes them fluid enough to recite or read aloud, as people did at the time of their writing. I've tried to avoid fancy words and tricks like poetic inversion, although in some cases I just couldn't help myself.

3. Preserve the rhythm and rhyme. The poems are wonderfully lyrical in the original Turkish, and I wanted to keep as much of that sound as I could. This type of structured verse has become less common in modern poetry, even though most people still love rhythm and rhyme (tune into any pop radio station for proof). I think this might partly explain the waning cultural importance of poetry.

4. Preserve the specific imagery. If I can satisfy all of the other priorities, I've tried to keep the surface meaning the same as the original, and this makes my job easier because Yunus's imagery is often inventive and memorable.

The poems refer to symbolism, scripture, legends, and spiritual figures that English-speaking readers are unlikely to be familiar with. I've resolved these in the following ways:

1. By adding a few words to give the reader some context (e.g., "Adhem...who left his throne to be a saint"). This is good because even without looking at the original, readers can easily dive deeper and learn about the people and ideas being referred to. The downside is that it uses up precious syllables and isn't always possible without breaking the form or the flow. When the references are to fairly well-known figures and ideas from Judaism, Christianity, and Islam, I've mostly left them as-is, only changing the names to their English-language or Arabic equivalents.

2. By translating into a parallel reference from the western canon (e.g., Layla and Majnun become "star-crossed lovers" in reference to Romeo and Juliet). These correspondences are rarely very exact, so I've used this method sparingly.

3. By translating the meaning as I understand it (e.g., for a reference to Dhu al-Qarnayn saying "ya," I interpreted this to be about him releasing Gog and Magog, and translated it into "demons at the end of days"). Here I've decided to sacrifice specificity to make the poems more widely accessible. I've also made sultans into kings, Sufis into mystics, and so on, both to make it easier for readers and easier for me, since the more traditional English words are easier to fit into a poem's structure. Of course, this makes the poems sound less exotic, but I think exoticism comes out of a mistaken fasci-

nation with the surface and not the substance. In Yunus's time, listeners would not have found anything exotic in these poems; it was just the ordinary world to them.

One word I haven't translated is "dervish," because the only close equivalent in English is "mendicant friar," which is really hard to fit into verse, and also doesn't convey that dervishes could get married and hold ordinary jobs. We have some other words like "mystic," "ascetic," and "monk," but I feel like each only captures part of what it means to be a dervish. Hopefully you'll either already be familiar with the word, do some research to become familiar with it, or just get the idea from the poems themselves. Dervishood encompasses a number of related spiritual paths, but I think that what Yunus meant by it would have included simple living or voluntary poverty, devotional practices like meditation, prayer, and fasting, and renunciation of the self and all worldly goals.

Indo-European languages like English divide the world into he, she, and it. Those of us who grew up speaking these languages are so entrenched in that way of looking at things that we rarely notice it, except when learning another Indo-European language with a different set of rules. Turkish and related languages are in a different family and mostly don't draw a gramatical distinction between male and female, living and nonliving. This leaves a certain ambiguity, and I've tried to preserve that ambiguity where possible because I feel it supports the universal nature of Yunus's message.

Cultural Parallels

When searching for imagery and culture from the western literary tradition to draw on, it's hard to find a single direct parallel to Yunus Emre. But looking within a few generations of his life, I can put together pieces of it from the culture of feudal Europe. In what is now Italy, Saint Francis of Assisi had dedicated his life to mysticism, renunciation of the world, and connection to God and nature. In what is now France, Guillaume de Machaut was composing haunting music full of longing for a seemingly impossible love. And in England, Geoffrey Chaucer was writing lucid verse with all the colorful vitality of the middle ages. Put these together and I think that's as close as I can get to describing the spirit of Yunus Emre. To learn about the life and legend of Francis of Assisi, I've drawn from Nikos Kazantzakis's beautiful *Saint Francis*. To catch the tone of longing, Machaut's music speaks to me with no need for words. For the poetic voice, Chaucer's English is unfortunately too distant to be much help. But since many of the early audience for Yunus's poetry would have been farmers, I've taken inspiration from Wendell Berry, America's own farmer-poet, particularly his earthy spirituality and plainspoken, unadorned style. Having grown up in a rural part of the American Southeast, I've drawn inspiration from that regional dialect, for example in expressions like "run your mouth" and "some folks." Hopefully these will come across to readers from other parts of the world.

About the Poetic Forms

The *ghazal* is an ancient poetic form that originated in Arabic and eventually spread to many other languages with an Arabic or Persian influence. Yunus wrote many poems in this form, some holding strictly to the form and some playing with it a little. The best way to illustrate the conventions is probably by example, so here's a short *ghazal* I've written as a demonstration:

> This world to cast my eyes about,
> too big to be so wise about.
>
> And me a tiny wooden boat
> that stormy seas will rise about.
>
> For seeking you I can't be still;
> a frightened bird still flies about.
>
> This ocean has more parting ways
> than we can say goodbyes about.
>
> The sailor, salt in all his pores,
> just shakes his head and sighs about.
>
> Our ancient wounds which have no name,
> a child feels and cries about.
>
> But sea without, and sea within,
> no surface to capsize about.
>
> What's Hinterlander hinting at
> that even silence lies about?

Notice the following points:

1. The poem is organized into couplets. Each couplet is supposed to stand on its own as a statement, or a statement followed by the "proof" of that statement.

2. The lines can be in any meter, with any number of syllables, as long as they are all the same. Here the meter is iambic tetrameter.

3. Many of the lines end in "about," which in this case is the refrain. The refrain can be just a word, as in this example, or a longer phrase.

4. Just before each refrain is the rhyme, which in this case sounds like "-ize." Both lines of the first couplet must end with this rhyme and the refrain, and so must the second line of every other couplet.

5. The final couplet has a special role, because it includes the poet's pen name, often gets more personal, and often emphasizes the poem's theme. Sometimes there will be a play on words with the pen name, for example in this case there's a play on "Hinterlander" and "hint." In the poems in this book, you might want to know that "*yunus*" also means "dolphin" in Turkish, so when the final couplet references diving into the sea, it's a play on words that's been lost in translation. If you think about it, this is a very clever way for poets to sign their work, because it's hard to remove or change the name without spoiling the poem's conclusion.

Another part of the *ghazal* tradition, which I haven't reproduced in the example above, is that poems usually have a theme of unrequited love, somewhat like the "courtly love" tradition in medieval Europe. However, in religious *ghazals* this love is meant as a metaphor for a seeker's intense longing for union with God. Common tropes are the garden, the *bulbul* (which I've translated as "nightingale"), and the rose. The garden can be seen as representing the world, with God as the gardener, the nightingale as the alter-ego of the poet, and the rose as representing the beloved, or the beauty of earthly forms.

One aspect of the *ghazal* that's nearly impossible to translate is the rhyme, because even for the shortest allowable poem with five couplets, you'd need to find a collection of six words that rhymed, and these are very unlikely to fit into the six rhymes of the original without straining the meaning. I've only managed to do this with trivial rhymes like "-ing" as in the poem I've titled *Spring*. Sometimes even the refrain presents a challenge because the word order is different in Turkish and English, and it won't always naturally go at the end of an English sentence. Sometimes it only gets through in a ghostly form as a repeated concept, for example in *The Hour of Death*, where all the refrain lines have something to do with talking.

The *semai* is a Turkish form of folk poem that's something like a *ghazal* with a specific meter and an internal rhyme scheme. You can imagine the couplets broken into quatrains, with each line having eight syllables, and the rhyme scheme is ABAB CCCB DDDB and so on. Often there is no rhyme in the "B" lines, and instead all of them are the same line repeated as a refrain. As in the *ghazal*, the final quatrain includes the poet's pen name. These would typically be sung to a tune. In a few cases I've used this kind of rhyme scheme even when it wasn't present in the original because I like the sound of it and because in a way it compensates for all the times when I failed to rhyme. For some poems, I've dropped the form entirely and translated into blank verse or free verse, which allows for a more conversational tone. While I was working on *Let Down Thy Veil*, the original reminded me so much of Shakespeare that I just had to turn it into an Elizabethan sonnet, even though a few couplets had to be dropped to get it down to fourteen lines. But one way or another, I think at least a little bit of the *ghazal* or *semai* spirit remains in all of the poems.

About the Source Material

Yunus wrote a lot of poems, hundreds of them, so many that I haven't even looked at them all, and here I've only been able to translate a few. I selected them mostly by looking for imagery and phrases that called out to me, because I have to be excited about what I'm doing for my work to be any good. Some poems dropped a lot of names, and I skipped them because most readers wouldn't know the names. Others seemed to be referencing doctrinal disputes, and I skipped them because after all these years, the point is either no longer disputed or highly controversial. The ones I was sorry to skip over were the riddle poems, which are fascinating, but it's just too hard for me to tell whether I've got the meaning right, and even if I understood, it might depend on deep wordplay that can't be translated. *Let There Be Separation* has a little bit of that flavor. In the end, I've included the poems I stumbled across and liked, and I hope you like them too. If you're a fan of Yunus Emre and there's a poem you wish were in this book, please let me know and maybe we can make a second volume.

I wish I could direct you straight to the source material for each poem, but unfortunately it's not easy to find an authoritative source that's easily accessible without ordering a book from Turkey. These poems were originally circulated by word of mouth, so they don't have official titles, and they appear in various versions depending on which compilation you look at. Over the years, some of the poems may have been changed, added to, or even composed by someone else in Yunus's style. The sources I've translated from have themselves been translated into more modern Turkish, which is another place for variations to creep in. I've decided to embrace the spirit of folk poetry, which is as messy as history itself, and not worry too much about it. But in case you do want to search for original text, the following list gives you a Turkish phrase that's characteristic of each poem, usually either the refrain or the first line.

Come See: gel gör beni aşk neyledi

Crying: bir gün ol Hazret'e karşu

Hey Loverboy: ey aşk eri aç gözünü

I Came: beni buraya yollayan

I Don't Have any Wish to Fly: gözüm seni görmek için

I Need It Back: gerek şimden geri

If That's the Way: n'olur ise ko ki olsun n'olusar

Inside of Me: Hak bendedir bende

Invocation: dağlar ile, taşlar ile

It Comes and Goes: aşkın odu ciğerimi

Going Home: bu dünyaya gelen kişi

Let Down Thy Veil: nikabı yüzünden bırak

Let There Be Separation: ko ikiliği

Life Slips Through our Fingers: canı yağmaya verdik

Lying Down: sabah mezarlığa vardım

Mine: Kabe ve büt iman benim

Oh Nightingale: niçin ağlarsın bülbül hey

One Word: bu dem yüzüm süre duram

Plundered: bu canım yağma olsun

Poison: dost ilinin haberin desem

Spring: gitti bu kış zulmeti, geldi bahar yaz ile

That Pearl: Hak bir gevher yarattı

The Hour of Death: ecel oku erdi cana

What's Wrong With Me: ne acep derdim var benim

You Can't: sen derviş olamazsın

You're the One for Me: bana seni gerek seni

About the Illustrations

When trying to decide how to illustrate this book, I immediately thought of Turkish culture's rich tradition of illuminated manuscripts and calligraphy. I took some inspiration from the style known as *tezhip*, but to keep the cost of the book down I decided not to use color. Each illustration is formed from a single line, never crossing itself, which you could see as a symbol of the unity of God and creation, the thread of life, the labyrinth, or the winding spiritual journey that Yunus describes so well. Scribes of the medieval world used to copy books by hand with ornate letters to start the chapters and fanciful pictures in the margins. We don't normally do that anymore, but I hope that making the book itself a little prettier can add something to the message and to your enjoyment of it.

About the Translator

What business do I have translating these poems? I'm not a scholar, a Turk, a Sufi, or even a Muslim. The only qualifications I have are a love and respect for Yunus Emre's work, a little skill at writing in verse, and the power of obsession. I started these translations just to deepen my appreciation for the poems, with no thought of publication, but it somehow turned into a burning passion. I've felt Yunus's spirit working its way deeper into my bones and my relationship with the eternal intensifying. So I've already been richly rewarded, but if these translations can help even one other person open their heart or draw closer to God, I'll be even more pleased. I know that I can't do Yunus's poems justice, but I hope that at least I haven't done them an injustice.

I'm certain to have made mistakes. But they don't need to be set in stone, and I'd like to make this a living work as long as I have the time and energy to maintain it. If you're in a position to catch mistakes or suggest improvements, please email me at:

jesse.crossen@gmail.com

Let me know what you're thinking, tell me how to credit you, and I'll try to include it in a future edition. Maybe one day these will be "folk translations." Or feel free to email me just to tell me how the poems strike you; I always love to meet people and hear about their lives. If you're interested in my original poetry, essays, stories, and travel writing, you can find them at:

https://hinterlander.substack.com

I hope you enjoy reading this book as much as I've enjoyed creating it!

Invocation

With the mountains, with the stones,
    let me call thy name my Lord
With the birds at dusk and dawn,
    let me call thy name my Lord
With the fish in waters deep,
    with the wilderness's deer,
With the sages praying "dear God,"
    let me call thy name my Lord
With the radiant face of Christ,
    with Moses climbing Mount Sinai
With staff in hand beneath the sky,
    let me call thy name my Lord
With the burdened sighs of Job,
    with the crying eyes of Jacob,
With Muhammad the beloved
    let me call thy name my Lord
With praise for all that you provide,
    with grace to bear what you decide,
With ceaseless prayer to burn my pride,
    let me call thy name my Lord
I have known the world's ways,
    I've left behind what rumors say,
Clear head, bare feet to feel the way,
    let me call thy name my Lord
Yunus listens to the tales
    of mourning doves and nightingales,
Truth is seeking servants still,
    let me call thy name my Lord

One Word

Facing into this moment I linger,
    each moment my new moon rises,
    each moment I spend in celebrations,
    my summers and winters fresh as spring.

Clouds can't cast a shadow
    on the light of my moon.
Moonlight pours down from the heavens
    and will never run dry.

It shines into the darkness.
From its deep furrow,
    the heart sends up a tender shoot.
Swelling with darkness and moonlight,
    how can the ground hold it?

How many times the moon has risen,
    never straying from its path.
How many have gazed up at it,
    and its brightness never dims.

From the ground I looked up at my moon,
    and saw what I wanted in the sky.
But me, I need to face the earth,
    to me the earth is chanting blessings.

My verses are not for the sun and moon.
For lovers, one word is enough.
If I don't say it to my beloved,
   my love will pile up and bury me.

As soon as I say this word,
   everyone will know I'm in love.
Even if I keep quiet,
   they'll see it shining in my face.

So what if you're in love Yunus?
God has many lovers.
You've seen the lovers praying,
   so get down on your knees
   and join them.

Spring

Dead and gone the dark of winter,
    summer's chasing after spring
Herbs have sprouted fresh and tender,
    playful winds are lingering
Pastures green and lush again,
    beds of roses blush again
Fragrant tunes composing in
    the music only reeds can sing
Pleasant rumours from a friend
    buzzing in the grove and garden
Secrets lovers comprehend
    the nightingales are warbling
Who has seen the wise old owl
    in a garden tame and tended
Noble storks chant raspingly
    their voices aren't the sweetest thing
Every stem is strung with pearls
    that a jeweler wouldn't buy
Partridges fly side by side,
    they only think of eating
Tame birds perch upon the hand,
    nightingales in roses land
Owls prefer the lonely ruins,
    falcons rise and spread their wings
Where there is a lone dead tree,
    vultures crowd like bourgeoisie
Parrots with a taste for sweets
    will find a cage to perch repeating

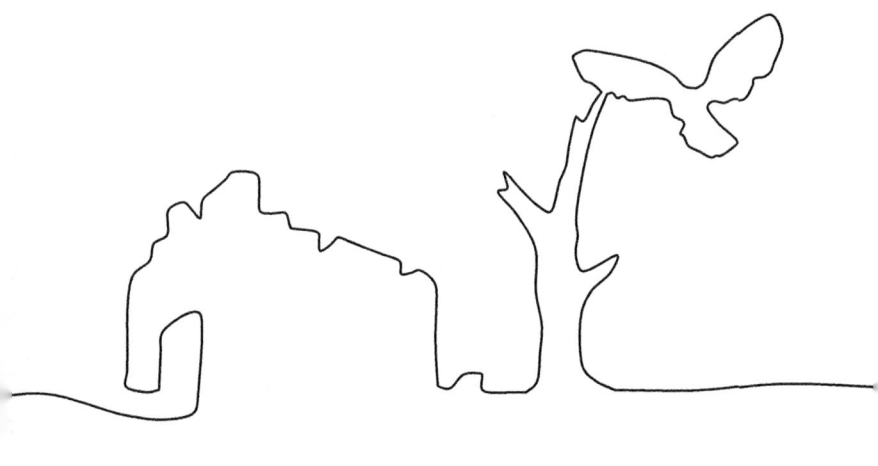

Every person has their key,
    the key that they were given
Believers have their catechisms,
    pious folks have praying
Doubters, fools, and hypocrites,
    thankful when they think of it
Lovers like to visit,
    and the clerics like their pleading
Dervishes should all know better,
    tongues are not for idle chatter
Best to put the house in order,
    Truth with Truth be gathering
"I'm a dervish," some will say,
    but they're making idle claims
If tomorrow's Judgement Day
    it's not God's face they're seeing
Being good won't get you far
    if you ever break a heart
To the holy land depart
    and maybe you'll find healing
Go to the almighty's house and
    ask if you can be a servant
There a sniffling beggar can
    be showered with a thousand blessings

Good folks know the world is good,
    crooks think that it's crooked
Liars can't believe the truth,
    tattletales like tattling
Some folks like to browse in shops,
    some like having nicer things,
Some need just a bit more cash,
    some their lives are frittering
Rich rewards of serving God,
    even kings can't take away
Nor demons at the end of days,
    with all the saints defending
Can't you see what Adhem saw
    who left his throne to be a saint?
In God's sight your stubborn pride
    is like a filthy rag you'd fling
Don't believe this fleeting world,
    don't believe it's yours to keep
Many who have said "it's mine"
    are shrouded corpses rotting
Drops of love fall from God's sky,
    rain to nourish thirsty hearts
Love's warm wind will blow away
    the bitter winter's frosty sting
Yunus, time to leave your sorrow
    you know nothing of tomorrow
We are born from the eternal,
    who can say what fate will bring?

It Comes and Goes

Your love has caught my heart on fire,
    the burning came, the burning goes,
Your love has turned me upside down,
    the spinning came, the spinning goes
I broke my heart and poured out blessings,
    when I came to love the King
Your chain of love my neck embracing,
    bondage came, the bondage goes
The faithful hold to what you say,
    but never dare to meet your gaze,
My eyes upon the Friend's kind face,
    the looking came, the looking goes
I must not step into the fight,
    or let my heart upset my head
And yet my eyes are wet with blood,
    the crying came, the crying goes
Oh, the nightingale is sighing
    from a soul that aches with longing
Oh my own poor heart is breaking,
    parting came, the parting goes
Lover Yunus speaks these verses
    nightingales make shrieking noises
Here the Friend has planted roses
    fragrance came, the fragrance goes

I Need It Back

Your love was raining on my heart
I need those raindrops back again
A flame has gone out in my soul
I need that burning back again

Back when I had fire and rain
I fed the stove, I reaped the grain
The sun plowed wrinkles on my skin
I need that sunlight back again

Down what strange paths my life has led
My heart hung heavy with regrets
And leaked and left me soaking wet
I need that bleeding back again

I had eyes so raw with weeping
Knees so bruised with constant kneeling
Looked up to the Friend, appealing
Bring that feeling back again

Once I knew I came to serve you
Knew the path of love and virtue
Knew my longing to deserve you
Bring that knowing back again

Once my heart cried out for yours
Each moment we were parted for
I beat my face against your door
I need to be like that again

Yunus once had crazy notions
Swam the sea and learned its motions
Found a pearl beneath the ocean
Dive and find that pearl again

That Pearl

Long ago God grew a pearl
    nestled in the folds of space
And with one majestic gaze
    it shattered into all creation

God made the seven folds of earth
    spreading out the pearly dust
Made the seven folds of heaven
    from the pearl's swirling mist

Poured out all the seven seas
    from the dewdrops on the pearl
Sculpted seafoam into mountains
    made them fast upon the ground

Out of love for living creatures
    made Muhammed as their teacher
Loved the ones believing in him
    made Ali to help defend them

Heaven knows what work it took
    the wisdom in our holy book
Yunus drank in ecstasy
    from that pearl from the sea

Let Down Thy Veil

Let down thy veil, allow me just one glimpse
I see the full moon shining from thy cheek
And from thy lips the honeyed light that drips
And from thy smile more sweet
    than sugar's sweet
Comes more than any mortal tongue could say
And part thy lips, among the coral beds
A string of pearls brighter than the day
That glimpse, that instant will not leave my head
And draws me like a moth to candle flames
I circle round thy light, I'm trapped, I'm hurt
I beg thee, don't release me from these chains
Without thy light my body's only dirt
Oh Yunus, join the flame, I'll set thee free
The light thou saw reflects God's light in thee

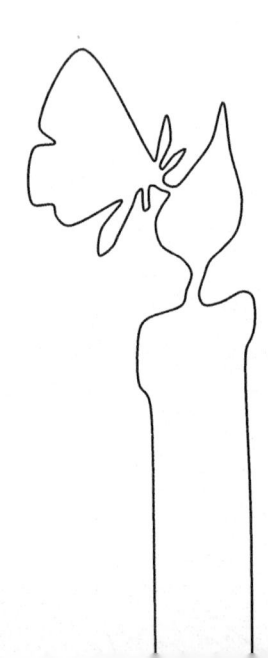

You're the One for Me

Your love welled up from deep within,
    you're the one for me I need you
Day and night it's spilling over,
    you're the one for me I need you
What wealth could ever make me glad,
    what poverty could make me sad
I'm too distracted with your love,
    you're the one for me I need you
Your love is even known to kill
    the fools who dive into your sea
With you their drowning lungs will fill,
    you're the one for me I need you
Your love's like wine, and I can't stop,
    passed out drunk on a mountaintop
Asleep, awake, my only thought
    is you're the one for me I need you
Mystics need some talk and laughter,
    workmen need the sweet hereafter
Star-crossed lovers need each other,
    you're the one for me I need you
And if your love should do me in,
    scatter my ashes to the wind
What's left of me will cry out then:
    you're the one for me I need you
Heaven, Heaven, say the churchmen,
    have some mansions, have some virgins
They can have them if they want them
    you're the one for me I need you
Yunus is what I've been named,
    each day that passes fans my flame,
In heaven and earth I want the same,
    you're the one for me I need you

Going Home

Those who came into this world
    should go again.
Here they're only guests,
    and they should go home someday.

Besides, before we left we promised
    to return and visit an old friend.
How long will we linger here?
    The time we've spent should be enough.

We'll arrive back home
    at just the right time for a visit.
When a traveller is sure of their destination,
    their heart should beat faster.

How can their heart not beat faster
    on the road to their homeland?
For people in love with life,
    this is the road they should travel on.

Why would a soul be planted here
    if it's not worthy of wisdom?
Why would the heart feel homesick
    if the tongue could explain it all?

I wonder what it's like back home…
If you could truly remember it,
    love would burst out of your head
    and set your heart to howling.

Yunus, tell us all about it now
    if you want to.
You're going home to marry your beloved,
    of course your heart is pounding.

Hey Loverboy

Hey loverboy, head in the clouds
Hey, now and then why not look down?
See graceful flowers on the ground
Here and gone within a season

Dressed in lovely summer gowns
They sway and bend among their kind
Now go and ask a craftsman whether
He could make just one so fine

From each flower's thousand graces
Learn to pray with upturned faces
From each bird whose sweet voice rises
Learn the way to sing God's praises

Study on God's might and power
Making ripe each fruit and flower
Surely in a lifetime we can
Understand the colors turning

Colors blooming day by day
To fall to earth and rot away
In this turning there's a lesson
Might be wise to pay attention

If you understood it more
Oh grief would shake you to the core
Such gut-deep grief to set you spinning
Shedding all your sins and winnings

What did you come here to do?
What will knowing things amount to?
When you've finished you will die
And love won't get you out alive

We all know people come and go
God puts us here and takes us back
Those drinking up love's honeyed wine
And everyone who hears these lines

Hey Yunus, these words smell like earth
You quit your playing in the dirt
If your words from God descended
There could be no evil in them

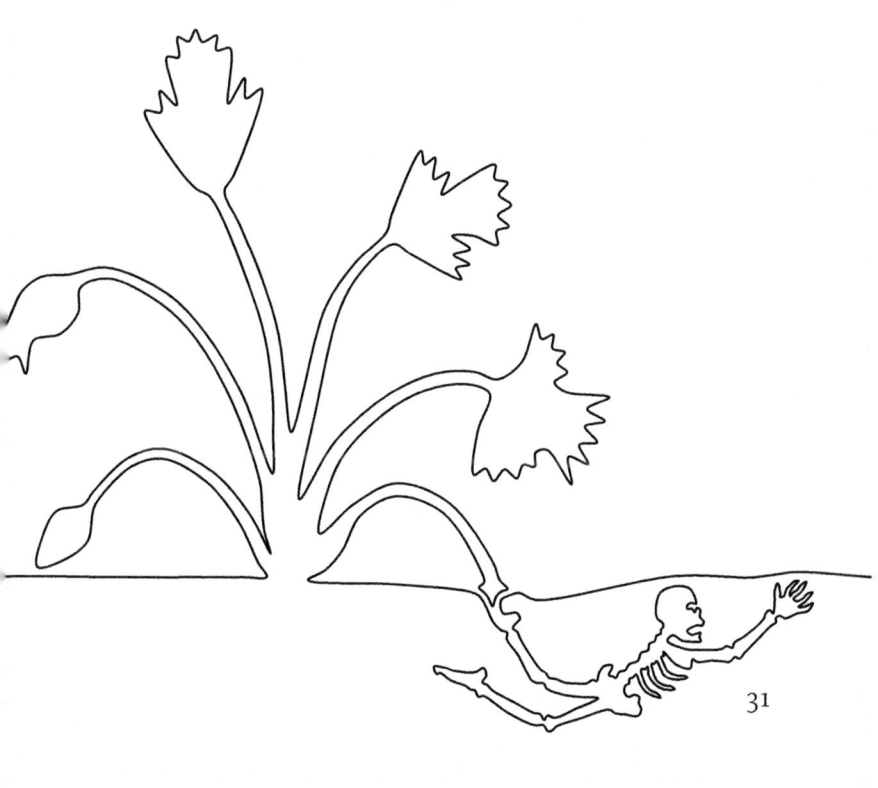

Lying Down

At dawn I reached a field of headstones,
    beds for corpses lying down.
They got too sick to cure and then
    their lifetime ended lying down.

Here a husband, here a soldier,
    here a lord, and here a leper
Spent their day for worse or better,
    darkness found them lying down.

I reached the graveyard in a hearse,
    looked up at death's almighty purse
That pays the dead their just deserts,
    and death was not yet lying down.

My neighbors with their chests caved in
    while maggots wandered on their skin,
And young girls with a child in them,
    sweet roses withered lying down.

They left behind unfinished work,
    their pearly teeth adorn the earth,
Their scattered hairs enlace the dirt,
    the ground embraced them lying down.

While bodies rot and reach their end,
    their souls reach out to find the Friend,
And don't you see you're one of them?
Our time has come for lying down.

Crying

One day I'll come before the Lord
On my knees and crying, crying
Death's messenger awaits my soul,
I hand it over crying, crying

The messenger will take my soul
All passed away, my life, my days
Condemned to moulder in a shroud
And all I'm good for's crying, crying

Pacing back and forth in darkness
Bloodshot eyes so wet and raw
One day into the shadowed grave
I will be lowered crying, crying

A waxen seal glues down my tongue
A weight is chained upon my arm:
The heavy book of all my sins
I hold it to me crying, crying

Lover Yunus, God means business
Sacrifice yourself to love
Faith is all our flesh can carry
I start praying, crying, crying

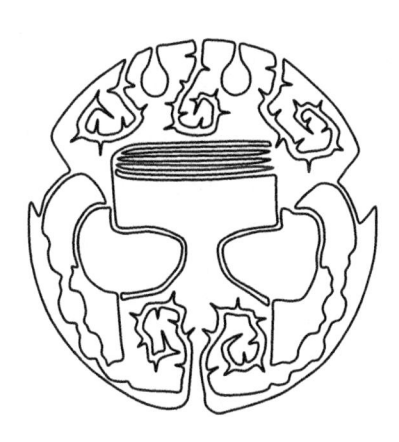

I Came

I was commanded to this world
Knowing I had work to do, I came
I had no choice but to obey
And so to do my work, I came

Many times I came to this world
Came to saints and siezed their garments
Found the mighty and renowned
And boiling over in their souls, I came

With words of strength I broke their will
My fire set their hearts ablaze
The secrets of this world were mine
To show them to the common folk, I came

I made Idris like a tailor,
    cutting teachings from the scriptures,
    pinning, stitching into garments
I taught Seth to be a weaver,
    spinning threads of holy law,
    on his loom they turned to scriptures
David sang resplendent psalms,
    when he cried out to me, I came

I came to love the moon's bright blade
Her keen edge dripping honeyed moonlight
I lost myself in her dark eye
To the shadow nestled
    in the crescent moon, I came

When Moses went upon the mountain,
    as the sacrificial ram,
    to walk beside him meek, I came
When Ali unsheathed his sword,
    through the broken city gates,
    to fight beside him brave, I came

Like the ocean to the shore
Like the bucket to the well
Like prayer to Jesus on the tongue
Thus to do my work, I came

In the full moon when it rose
In the cloud hung from the sky
In the raindrop when it fell
In the sunbeam when it shone, I came

By rumors told to passersby
By inspirations shown to pilgrims
By revelations made to seekers
By hidden signs in dreams, I came

Mine the only cure for suffering
Mine the art of sculpting flesh
Mine the lineage of Moses
And to meet him on the mount, I came

Now my path has come to you
Who have learned to call me Truth
When your tongue rang with my name
You spoke of me, you thought of me, I came

POISON

Friend, if I bring you news of your homeland,
    will you believe it?
Fellow traveler, when you know the way there,
    will you take it?
You can travel back there by magic,
    just put some poison in your wine.
When you can't hold the cup of poison anymore,
    won't you stop drinking?
Once your hand is dead,
    it can't hold onto suffering.
If it was made into a sweetmeat just for you,
    would you taste the poison?
Back home there is no sun and moon,
    no way to count the days and months.
If you could leave your troubles behind,
    would you need to count the days?
If you could leave yourself behind,
    fall into the hands of emptiness,
    drink from the pure ecstasy of love,
    wouldn't you drop all this earthly baggage?
This body of yours is just a pattern
    of fire, wind, earth, and water.
Yunus, think about the essence,
    is it just water and earth you're made of?

Let There Be Separation

With nobody else around,
    you can't get offended
Stay on dry land,
    and you'll never find a pearl
You can't walk on the road
    unless somebody cleared it for you
The full moon can only rise
    when the sun sets
A listener won't catch your drift
    if they're a fool
A heart cannot be pierced
    if it's made out of stone
If your walking stick breaks in two,
    it won't go back together
That's how it is!
    No ointment will heal it
A traveler sets out to cross the desert,
    it looks easy standing in the shade
Let there be separation,
    you'll have oneness soon enough
One soul separated from all the others
    can't settle down
Yunus, give your soul
    to the path of Truth
If you don't give your soul,
    you'll never find your beloved

You Can't

Dervishood has said to me
You can't become a dervish
Even riding on my back
You can't become a dervish

Openhearted, feeling deep
A dervish must prepare to weep
Must be gentle as a sheep
You can't become a dervish

Must be handless when attacked
Must be cussed and not talk back
Must give up the will to act
You can't become a dervish

Run your mouth with empty praise
All those words get in your way
Yelling when they won't obey
You can't become a dervish

On this path, if yelling helped
Then Muhammed would have yelled
You've been known to yell yourself
You can't become a dervish

If you fail to get it right
If you fail to find a guide
If destiny's not on your side
You can't become a dervish

Dervish Yunus come here now
Dive into the sea right now
If you don't dive in the sea
You can't become a dervish

What's Wrong With Me

Dervishes and brothers, hey!
I wonder what is wrong with me.
When people see my love drunk ways,
They wonder what is wrong with me.

No dervishes can be ashamed,
No lovers can be playing games,
No doctors cure what they can't name,
They wonder what is wrong with me.

Your ocean waves that crash and sweep,
My longing burned my heart so deep,
This hole in me makes people weep,
And wonder what is wrong with me.

My Lord, I dove into this pain,
Dove deep into your love's domain.
Against your waves I swim in vain,
And wonder what is wrong with me.

Lover Yunus, you dove again,
Dove straight into this mess you're in,
And entered truth, your only home,
I wonder what is wrong with me.

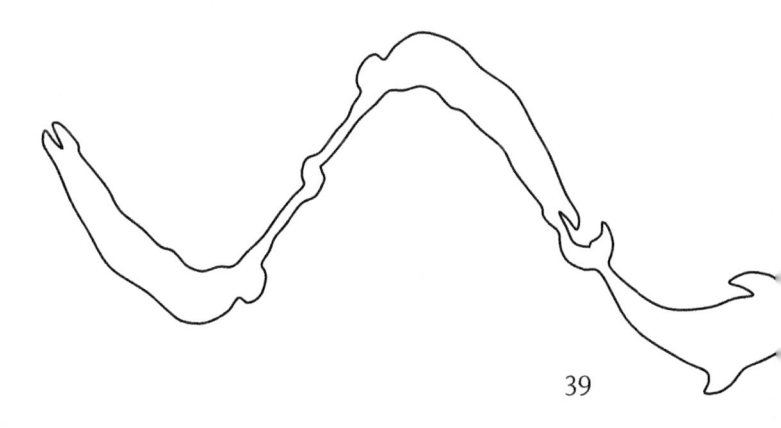

Come See

My reckless heart dreamed up this love
Come see what love has done to me
My head thinks twice and won't give up
Come see what love has done to me

My tears roll down in tracks of sadness
Love has painted me with blood
Is this wisdom, is this madness
Come see what love's done to me

I walk and walk despairingly
I dream the Friend is there with me
Wake up and fall upon my knees
Come see what love has done to me

Your love has cast a spell on me
A sickness come to dwell in me
I think it plans on killing me
Come see what love has done to me

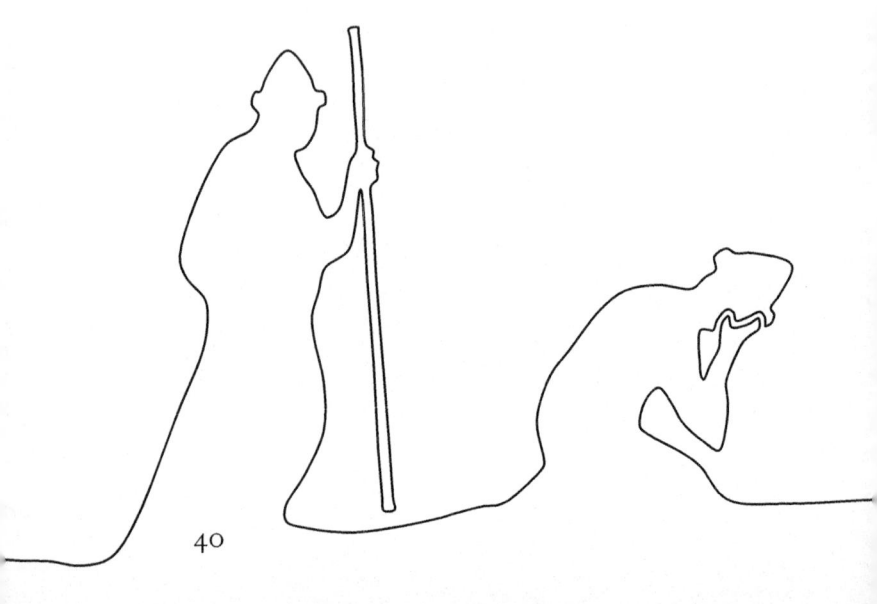

Sometimes like the winds I blow
Sometimes dusty as the roads
Sometimes like the floods I flow
Come see what love has done to me

Your waters flow, eternal fountains
My heart aching for my mountains
Feet that walk in two directions
Come see what love's done to me

My face is pale, my eyes are wet
My shattered heart, my guts upset
My worried friends begin to fret
Come see what love has done to me

Poor old Yunus, tired and poor
From head to foot an open sore
Wandered far from your friend's door
Come see what love has done to me

The Hour of Death

Now your hour of death has come,
the rest walk on without a word.
"How careless to get left behind,"
those who came prepared are saying.

Don't you remember, says the Ruler,
what job I sent you here to do?
I trusted you with life and soul,
and all you bring me is this talking.

Your soul is yanked away from flesh,
your upright I slumps down and falls,
the jewels within your eyes spill out.
"How did it come to this?" you say.

Well, you walked through life so prideful,
your name was written in the book.
This house of earth is low and level,
come now, sinner, come in and talk.

"Wait, is this my grave?" you say,
"Where are the rewards I looked for?"
Did you show up empty-handed?
Creeping, crawling, grasping, talking?

Your cleverness led you astray;
without my Lord your evil tongue
has sent you to a shallow grave
in this place of desolation.

If you'd been among the faithful,
you could say "goodbye, goodbye,"
and angels would fly down to earth
to fill your grave with words of glory.

Yunus stop it with this worry,
the day will come for you to rest.
God will give you one more blessing:
Come to heaven, come in and talk.

If That's the Way

Let it happen, if that's the way
Be one with God if that's the way
The sea of love has flowed with blood
Jump right in if that's the way
It drowns its swimmers so they say
Let it kill you if that's the way
The afterlife will never end
Stay forever if that's the way
One day your well will fill with dirt
Let it fill if that's the way
Some folks sit upon high horses
Let them ride if that's the way

Mine

The faith in shrine and idol, mine
Men broken on the wheel are mine
The passing cloud, the shooting star
The rain that turns to snow are mine

Summer-bringer paints the colors
Sows the seeds in hearts of lovers
Proud forefathers and foremothers
They who live to serve are mine

Birdsong when the thunder passes
Heads that swell with shouts and curses
Fattening among the grasses
Crawls a viper that is mine

To Hamza from the farthest shores
Came footsoldiers for holy wars
To topple scores of pagan lords
His cunning and his zeal are mine

Winding flesh on bony spindle
Knitting skin, with life I kindle
Wisdom sleeping in the cradle
Strength that flows from breasts is mine

Well my true love, since you've come
I will show you where it starts
The road that leads into the heart
They who stay and never part are mine

Calling mine the skies and valleys
Calling mine the west and east
And summoning the seven seas
My name is Yunus and the ocean's mine

Inside of Me

God's in the village square,
    like me a traveller.
I feel it in the air,
    God is inside of me.

Suffering apart from you,
    I hid my heart from you.
Cleansing my inner truth,
    God is inside of me.

What if my house burns down,
    won't leave a scar on me.
Walking on poisoned ground
    won't be the death of me.

That God's apart from me,
    that I cannot believe.
I have searched endlessly,
    God is inside of me.

Life is a prison cell,
    we're doing time in it.
Prayer is our water well,
    faith is the bread we get.

Preachers stop by to preach,
    selling delicious treats.
I have enough to eat,
    God is inside of me.

So close to God though, won't it
 burn you, Yunus?
Won't your heart that can't stop bleeding
 drain you, Yunus?
What will serving forty years
 return you, Yunus?
I hid away my diamonds,
 God is inside of me.

What the Prophet taught us won't
 forsake you, Yunus.
Hold yourself apart and God can't
 take you, Yunus.
Just let Mohammed's light
 illuminate you, Yunus.
I embraced eternity,
 God is inside of me.

Oh Nightingale

Are you a stranger to this place?
Oh nightingale why do you cry?
Did you grow tired and lose your way?
Oh nightingale why do you cry?

Have you crossed over desert sands?
Fought the mountain's snowy winds?
Did you get parted from your friend?
Oh nightingale why do you cry?

Alas, how cruel the fates can be
I wish that I could bring you peace
Is it your friend you long to see?
Oh nightingale why do you cry?

Did your nest and eggs all tumble?
Did it leave you crushed and humbled?
Did your friend leave you in trouble?
Oh nightingale why do you cry?

Once you summered in the gardens
Roses picked with dew still on them
Now you're desperate and downtrodden
Oh nightingale why do you cry?

From dreams I cried myself awake
And all my skin was stripped away
My heart was charred and still ablaze
Oh nightingale why do you cry?

Where did the one called Yunus go?
He followed God and drowned in love
And now the spring has come once more
Oh nightingale why do you cry?

I Don't Have any Wish to Fly

My eyes are for beholding you
My hands for reaching out to you
Today my soul goes seeking you
I hope tomorrow finding you

Today my soul goes seeking you
Tomorrow you'll give me my voice
Your heaven's what I'm longing for
I don't have any wish to fly

To fly to heaven, so they say
To that reward the faithful chase
With virgins lounging round the place
I have no lust for their embrace

You gave me so much already
(Doubly blessed with son and daughter)
Even this desire has left me
Let me run away with you

Give devotees your memory
It's you I want, it's you I need
These days I don't even care
To sit here in my rocking chair

I've been longing for your presence
As you long to show your essence
In your work there is no cruelty
Making this world as it should be

Life Slips Through our Fingers

We were given life in water
Life pours out between our fingers
Jewels will dazzle moneychangers
While the gold slips through their fingers

I am like a careless merchant
Never minding my accounting
How can I expect a profit?
Losses slipping through my fingers

But on this road, that's only wise
The dead can't carry merchandise
It's only naked souls can rise
And let the world slip through our fingers

On this road it's hard to tell
Both good and evil wear a veil
We stop and flirt with blasphemy while
Faith is slipping through our fingers

You build this castle round your soul
You're always working, stacking stones
But when the walls no longer hold,
"You" and "me" slip through our fingers

We walk through the crowded market
Nothing left inside our pockets
No more urge to buy, we've lost it
Time is slipping through our fingers

After all these many seasons
Oh how Yunus understands it
Lose your pride and you will ripen
Struggle slipping through your fingers

51

Plundered

I have found the soul of souls
Let this soul of mine be plundered
Gone beyond all gains and losses
Let this shop of mine be plundered

I gave up my selfish ways
Tore the veil from off my face
Fell into the Friend's embrace
Let these doubts of mine be plundered

I gave up on being me
The Friend devoured my property
And I became a landless gypsy
Let my worldly goods be plundered

I got tired of being a loner
Dressed up fancy like a lover
Got mixed up with tavern brawlers
Let this strength of mine be plundered

Lonely creatures searched in fright
The Friend came to us in the night
To fill our ruined hearts with light
Let this world of mine be plundered

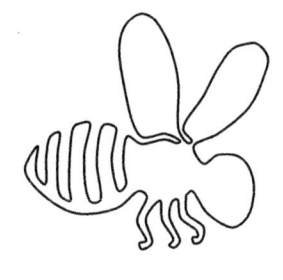

I got tired of endless cravings
Spinning through the wheel of seasons
I have found the queen of gardens
Let my little plot be plundered

A friend and I got in a fight
I ran back to apologize
Gave in and took love's good advice
Let my own advice be plundered

Yunus you've been talking sweet,
What honeyed candy did you eat?
I've found the most delicious honey
Let this hive of mine be plundered

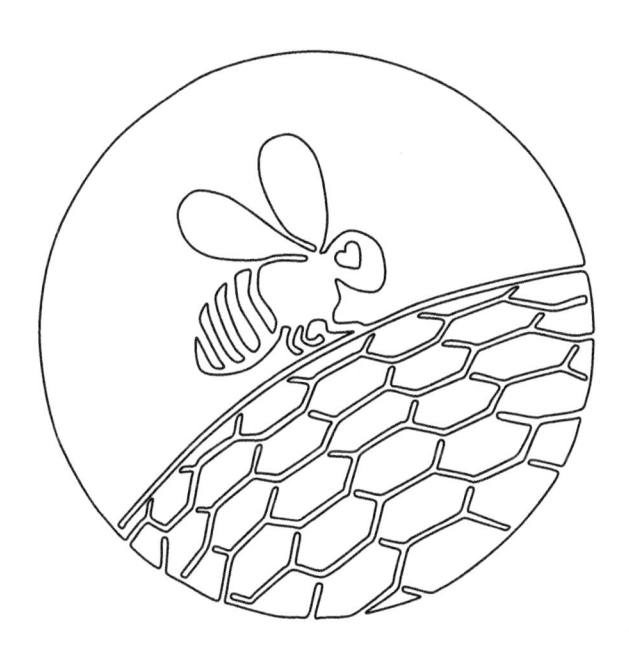

Thanks

Thanks to God for this wonderful world. Thanks to Yunus Emre for channeling God's love and humanity's struggles. Thanks to my family, my friends, and all my many teachers for raising and nurturing my body, mind, and spirit. Thanks to Tyler for helping me up from a dark place and setting me on the road to something bigger. Thanks to Sally and Tim for revealing the juice in the spiritual path and the juice in endless exploration. Thanks to Jerry and Carol Anne for telling me about Yunus Emre. Thanks to the Echo Chamber and the Lauras for being an early audience and offering moral support. Thanks to Sadie for proofreading this book. And thanks to you for reading it!

Tools and Resources

Translation:

- TurEng (excellent general-purpose dictionary)
- Wiktionary (good for etymology and grammar)
- Reverso Context (good for usage and idioms)
- The glossary from Yunus Emre's *Divan* compiled by Dr. Mustafa Tatcı
- *www.nedirnedemek.com* (more obscure words)
- *nedir.ileilgili.org* (regional and archaic words)
- Google Translate (sparingly for gestalt meaning)
- Wikipedia (for background research)

Versification: RhymeZone, *www.powerthesaurus.org*

Typesetting and Design: LuaLaTeX, ImageMagick

Illustrations: Skedio, Inkscape

Typefaces: All text is set in Whitman by Kent Lew, except for Turkish text which is set in Noto Serif.